CREATIVITY IN PAPER

A Sourcebook for Teachers and Parents

by Masami Hanamura and Wendy Jones

Creativity in Paper
A Sourcebook for Teachers and Parents

by Masami Hanamura and Wendy Jones © 1993
Published by Graphic-sha Publishing Co,.Ltd. © 1993

This book was designed and produced by
Graphic-sha Publishing Co.,Ltd.
1-9-12 Kudan-kita Chiyoda-ku Tokyo 102 Japan

All works were specially created for this book by
Masami Hanamura.
Text written by Wendy Jones
Book design and art direction by Ken'ichi
Yanagawa
Typeset by Yosho Insatsu Co.,Ltd.
Printed in Japan by Kinmei Printing Co.,Ltd.
Tokyo Japan

ISBN4-7661-0722-5

Table of Contents

FORWARD

Masami Hanamura

When I was young there were still lots of fish, birds and insects in Tokyo.

The city was rich in nature. As a boy I was especially fond of catching insects and fishing, and spent my days playing in this way, completely absorbed from morning to night. Perhaps I can still say this about myself.

But to my regret, this is not true of my children. They are not so interested in bugs and fish.

Last summer I went with them to Hakone. We were standing on the bank of the Hayakawa river watching the ayu fisherman when suddenly a big Oniyanma approached and buzzed around us. My children watched in wonder until the dragonfly flew away. A moment later, one of them said: "That dragonfly had big, green eyes!"

For myself, I was struck by the fact that ever since boyhood I have been thrilled to see an Oniyanma dragonfly.

This is the third book in a series I have authored, and in it many dragonflies and other kinds of bugs appear. In order to make it more useful in classrooms and homes we have included many diagrams, explanations and ideas which show how to create and enjoy these paper creatures. We hope it contributes to the growth of your children's sensitivity, dreams and energy, as well as to communication between yourself and your children.

Wendy Jones

When I first started working in Day Care teaching two and three year olds, I was amazed at the large variety of pattern books available for teachers to use to incorporate art projects into their lesson plans.

Although the pattern books were great, they all lacked an important ingredient: how to use them in display and design to brighten up the classroom and how to spark the interest and expand the imagination of children of all ages.

This book is designed to do just that. Inside you will find page after page of ideas and what to do with them. Included are ideas to incorporate art projects into your lesson plans, bulletin boards, learning centers, etc. There are also different ways to display the children's art work and how to liven and brighten up the classroom and make it inviting and exciting for the children.

This book is dedicated to my Dad who helped me take the first "li" and to my Mom who helped me believe it was possible.

GETTING ORGANIZED

Teachers and parents know how much smoother the day goes when everything is ready and waiting for the children. Nothing frays nerves faster than a room full of children who have nothing to do.

Formulate a plan and expand on basic ideas to give new meaning to the mundane. Gather your supplies and use them to the fullest. Adding texture and dimension will make an ordinary art project more interesting.

When decorating your room make it colorful and dramatic. Who said elephants had to be grey, or bears had to be brown?

Children love to be involved and to help in the projects. Take a basic theme and make it wild and exciting.

Don't underestimate the parents. Although many parents today are both working, they love to help when they can. Scraps of material, paper towel rolls, oatmeal containers, egg cartons, etc., can all be used to liven up the room. Don't hesitate to send home a note and give them an opportunity to be involved. Most welcome the chance to help out. ABOVE ALL, HAVE FUN!

ENJOY!

How to Use This Book

The mother and baby chameleon

Materials required

Scissors, paper cutter, glue or adhensive for
paper, tweezers, pencil, cellophane tape,
tracing paper, colored paper, paper that you
have dyed yourself, photographs, newspaper,
tag board or cardboard, cut cloth, tree leaves,
cutting paper, and so forth.

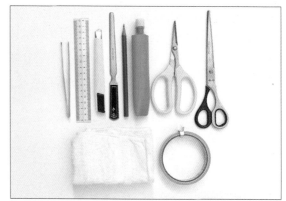

Duplicating the patterns in this book is easy. Using this mother and baby chameleon as an example, here is how to do it. First draw the basic outline of the mother in pencil in the size that is desired.

Next, add the details such as the eyes, mouth, hands, stomach, baby, etc.

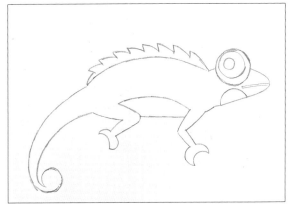

If desired, you can color in the design in the colors of your choice to see the completed copy.

After the colors and details are completed, use a piece of tracing paper to copy the outlines of the different pieces. To make a permanent pattern, transfer these pieces to tag board or cardboard.

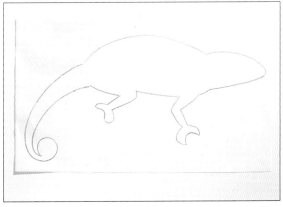

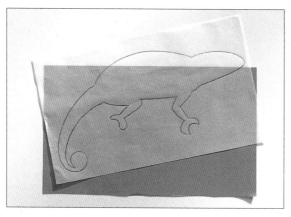

Place the different pieces on the desired colored construction paper.

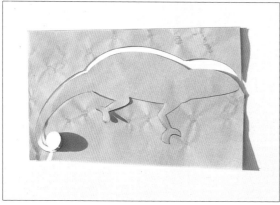

Cut out the pattern along the outline of the paper.

Apply glue to the reverse side of the paper.

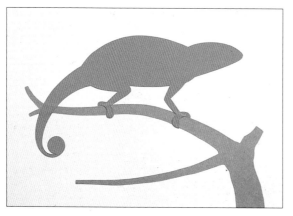

Next, glue the pattern onto your foundation paper if you plan to use one.

After cutting and pasting the main body, apply eyes in the same way.

Next, make the spine, throat details, and attach.

After making the mother chameleon, add the baby in the same way.

When the larger parts are completed add the finishing details. Then you're finished.

This same technique can be used to copy any of the pictures in this book.

CHAPTER 1

ANIMALS

Animals are a large part of our world and children of all ages love to learn about them.

Rather than have everyone in the class make the same animal why not break them down into groups of two or three and have a jungle of animals, or an ocean of fish. When displaying the work, creating an interesting scene is easier with a variety of animals.

In direct contrast, basic silhouettes can create a dramatic effect. Some of the children can paint the pictures of the lions, cut from butcher paper, while others can do the background using construction paper, paint, or tissue paper.

Adding finishing touches such as branches and grass will make a wall a giant bulletin board. Not only have the children practiced the cutting and gluing skills, they can see a project through to a conclusion.

Dimension and Display

Adding dimension, such as eye lashes or fur, is easy once you know how.

You can turn an ordinary picture into a dramatic art project by adding eyelashes or eyelids. The change is subtle but they make a masterpiece!

It may take a little extra time but the end results are fantastic.
You can also add dimension by using "Easter Grass" for background cover or plastic wrap over blue construction paper to give it a wet look.

For a dramatic difference use real branches or leaves found by you or the children during a nature walk. Vines can be created by using twine.

Don't forget to add leaves to the vines and hang the monkey from the vines!

For a different approach to an art project, use old scraps of wall paper or gift wrap for the body of the animal. Then the colors are more dramatic and can be easily achieved, and the outcome is striking.

By tearing the paper rather than cutting it you can make it more realistic. Notice also that brown paper bags have been used rather than brown construction paper. Features can be painted on as well as glued on.

Another way to display the lion, as you can see on the next pages, is to have the children make the faces and then add them to the painted bodies.

The bodies can be created by a very simple technique. Have the children use various colors of magic markers on pieces of white construction paper. Next spray the paper with water so the colors run together to create a mirage of colors.

Using newspaper, which is easy to get from the children, or from your own pile at home, you can transform it into this roaring lion with a little construction paper and imagination. For added fun use yarn for the mane rather than construction paper.

If you are feeling particularly daring you can let the children pick their own colors for the lions and tell them to use their own wild imagination. The results can be quite remarkable. Who ever heard of a lion with a green mane or a lion with a blue nose? The children can laugh and enjoy the different combinations of lions and even vote as to "the most colorful", or "the wildest looking". Make some ribbons and display them with the winners.

Taking a basic pattern you can make it as simple or as elaborate as you want depending on the age of the children and their ability.

Bulletin Boards

Make your room inviting! Entrance ways can be decorated to welcome and excite eager learners. Make this cat "door size" and hang up a saying like:

"Right this way for a purrr-fect day!!!!"

$J^{u}{}^{m}{}_{p}$ *into learning!!!!*

Another way to make your room inviting is to make the hallway outside your room bright and cheerful.

"Adventure is wating around the next bend!!!!"

Birthday Announcements

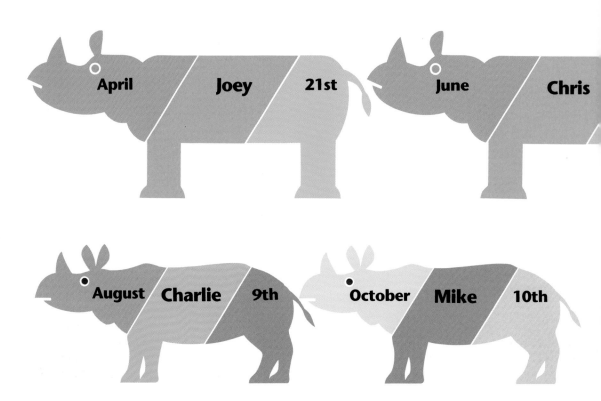

Rather than use the traditional cake and candles or clowns and balloons to display the children's birth dates, why not use a parade of rhinos instead? You can then use contrasting stripes or patterns to liven the picture up. Then write the dates and child's name on the stomach and write the month on the head.

Connect them together by their tails to form a chain of Rhinos!

The same principle can be used with the goats below. Write the month on the paper and the names and dates on the goat's belly. Make each goat a different color and then connect them.

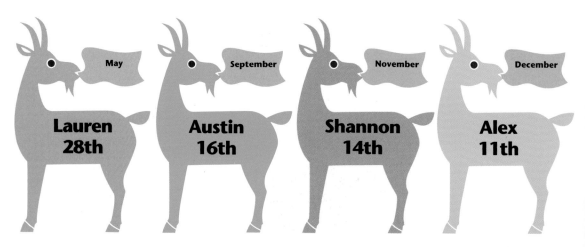

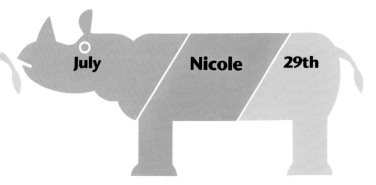

Whatever animal you choose be sure that it is bright and colorful. This activity will help the children learn the months of the year and they will love seeing their birthdays displayed on the wall!

Another idea is to use a different animal for each month. Have the children make each animal. The children will learn the names of the month by association and the display will brighten up the room.

Animal Alphabets

It's easy to purchase premade displays for the alphabet and some are quite elaborate. Think of how excited the children will be to help create a different animal for each letter in the alphabet? Upper and lower case letters can be written on the bodies of the animals and by using mothers and their babies, or by varying the size of the animal you can show the association.

On the next few pages I have given some examples of animals you can use.

W

W

C

c

D

d

Display these above the blackboard or at eye level for the children. Let them copy the letters onto the animals. The younger children may need to practice first.

Color Charts

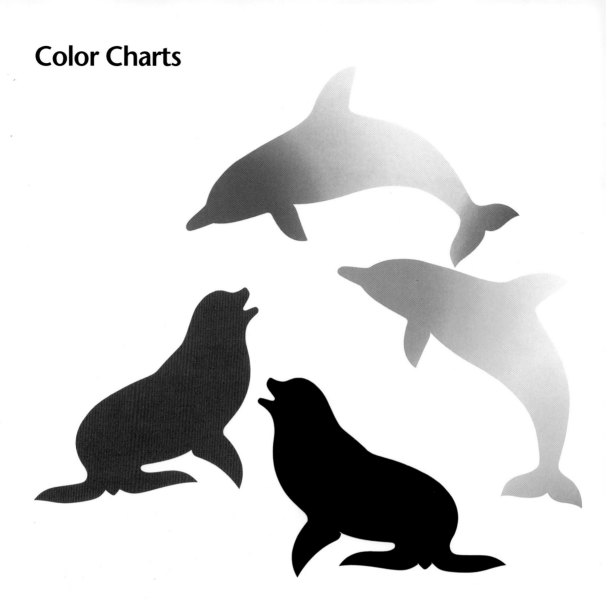

Children can display primary and secondary colors by making funny animals from different colored construction paper. The children can also make companion animals by changing the colors or patterns of the animals.

28

By having the children make the animals the benefits are two-fold. Children can easily remember the blue lizard or the pink cat they made, and the room has the added color. Note: You may have to cut out the patterns for the younger children but encourage the older ones to take their time and complete it themselves.

See how your room is taking shape! Pat yourself on the back and take a deep breath. You're almost finished!!

Number Charts

A good way to involve the children is to have them help make up number charts. There are a number of ways in which to make a simple number line or chart exciting to help the children and make them want to learn.

Start with a basic theme, such as the one below, and as the children master the concept of the numbers, add flowers to the bulletin board.

A variation of the same idea is to put addition, subtraction, multiplication, and division problems on the center of each flower. Change them periodically as the children master the problems. Put up a chart and encourage the children to participate. Mark the names with stars as they master the skills.

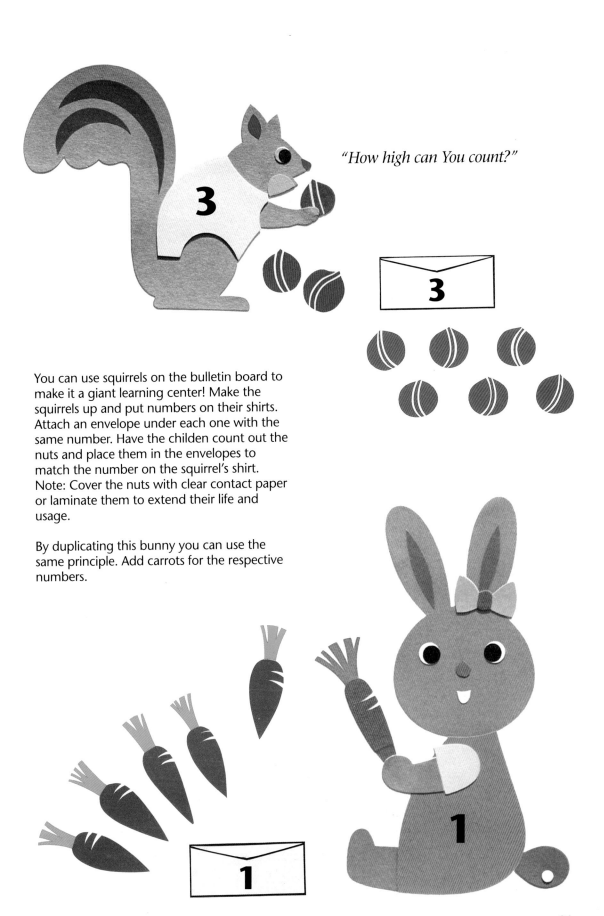

"How high can You count?"

You can use squirrels on the bulletin board to make it a giant learning center! Make the squirrels up and put numbers on their shirts. Attach an envelope under each one with the same number. Have the childen count out the nuts and place them in the envelopes to match the number on the squirrel's shirt. Note: Cover the nuts with clear contact paper or laminate them to extend their life and usage.

By duplicating this bunny you can use the same principle. Add carrots for the respective numbers.

By enlarging the snakes below you can encourage the children to learn their numbers in a new way.

Make sure to add more sections to the snakes as the children's ability increases. Write their names on the bulletin board and date them to show the children how they have improved.

You can use your bulletin board as an introduction to math when the children come into the room. Under this picture of the snake have a caption that reads:

By using your imagination and you can come up with silly sayings!

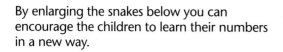

"Sssslipin' into math!"

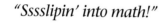

"Can you count my ssssectionss?"

Easy Puzzles

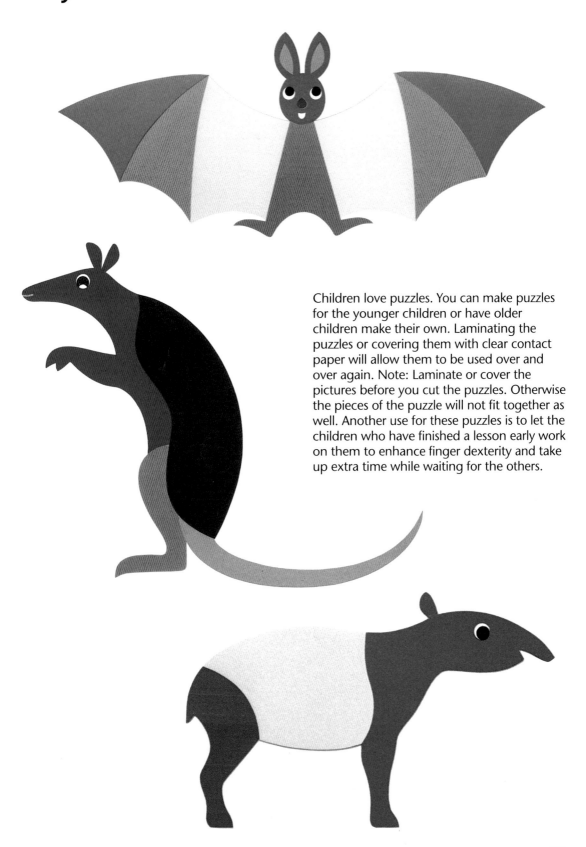

Children love puzzles. You can make puzzles for the younger children or have older children make their own. Laminating the puzzles or covering them with clear contact paper will allow them to be used over and over again. Note: Laminate or cover the pictures before you cut the puzzles. Otherwise the pieces of the puzzle will not fit together as well. Another use for these puzzles is to let the children who have finished a lesson early work on them to enhance finger dexterity and take up extra time while waiting for the others.

By cutting these pictures along the color lines, it makes it very easy to create fast puzzles.

Once the puzzles are mastered, you can have races with several puzzles to see who can do it the fastest.

Matching Games

Another fun game that is a time filler is matching animals. Make one of the animals bright and colorful and a copy of the same animal in a black silhouette. Or you could make them in light and dark shades to have the children learn "same and different". As always cover or laminate them. Store them in a large envelope or folders with the sides taped or stapled shut for easy access.

Another variation of this game is to use companion animals.

39

By mounting or drawing the animals on 4x6 index cards and letting the children color them, you can make another game for the children to enjoy. Attach several cards together by punching four holes along the top of the cards. Slip small rings through the holes to form a small notebook. *Next cut the cards 3/4 of the way up through the body of the animal, leaving a small border at the top of the cards. Make sure all of the animals are facing the same direction and are approximately the same size.

On the next few pages you will find more examples of animals you can use. The key is to decide where to make the cut.

42

Display the animals standing up rather than on all four legs for a different view. Punch the holes along the side of the cards instead of along the top. Proceed in the same way as before. The children will come up with a wide range of zany combinations. Another way to use this same principle is to have every child make the same animal and color them as they wish. Then when the children make the combinations the animals will all be the same but in different colors. They will really enjoy themselves!

If you keep the cards whole, you can group the animals (ie:zoo animals, jungle animals, etc.) and let the children make up their own notebooks to keep and play with at home.

Coloring Contests

Have a coloring contest - encourage the children to take their time and use lots of colors. Here are a few pictures to give you ideas of how you can turn ordinary pictures into colorful masterpieces.

Display a variety of the children's art work on a wall outside the room to create a giant collage. Have each of the children pick their best piece of art work to add to the collage.

CHAPTER 2
INSECTS

Children love BUGS! Some children are scared
of them but all are fascinated with insects.
Here are a few colorful butterflies to help the
children loose their fear and learn all about
the wonderful varieties of insect life.

Using these butterflies you can create a
dramatic mobile. From the simple to the
complex you can encourage even the
youngest children to use their imagination, as
on the next page.

Remember to use bright, cheerful colors. You
can hang the butterflies in groups, or clusters
or you can hang them alone all around the
room.

Mobile

For children with stronger artistic ability, you can use a more elaborate design of a butterfly and let them do the outline in black construction paper and fill the insides with multi-colored tissue paper or construction paper.

Not only will the children have dramatic results using this technique but they also learn about mobiles and two-dimensional art. Remind the children to cut out a front and a back so that when it is hung from the ceiling, it will be beautiful from any angle!

These dragonflies can be added to your mobiles or suspended from the ceiling with string. Make the bodies from construction paper and use tissue paper to give the wings a translucent look and quality.

Another way to make the dragonfly is to use craft clothes pins and paint them for the bodies. Make the wings from construction paper and glue to the body. Then make the eyes from Q-tips dipped in black paint. Cut the dipped end of the Q-tip off and glue on the figure to make the eyes stand up.

Collections

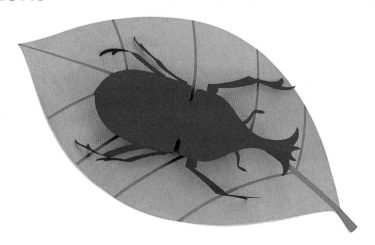

Beetles come in a variety of shapes and colors. They can be made by the children after they have had a field trip to a nearby nature center or natural museum. This will enhance the learning process and let the children have fun creating their own "collection" of beetles.

Some beetles can be hung from the leaves of a construction paper tree that can be erected in the corner of the room for a dramatic and eye catching display.

By using the illustration below you can create two dimensional insects to "stand up" on a nearby shelf or empty desk. Enlarge the illustration and tranfer it to a folded piece of construction paper. You can use colored construction paper or white paper and let the children color the beetles and cut them out. Note: Some of the younger children may need help cutting out the beetles' legs. Fold down the legs and display them for everyone to enjoy. On the next few pages there are some examples of colors and types of beetles.

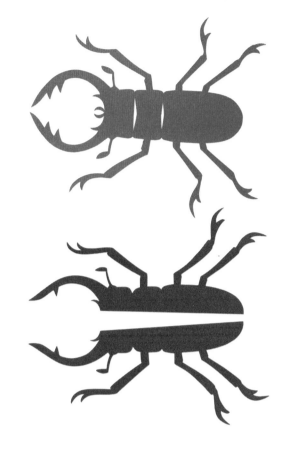

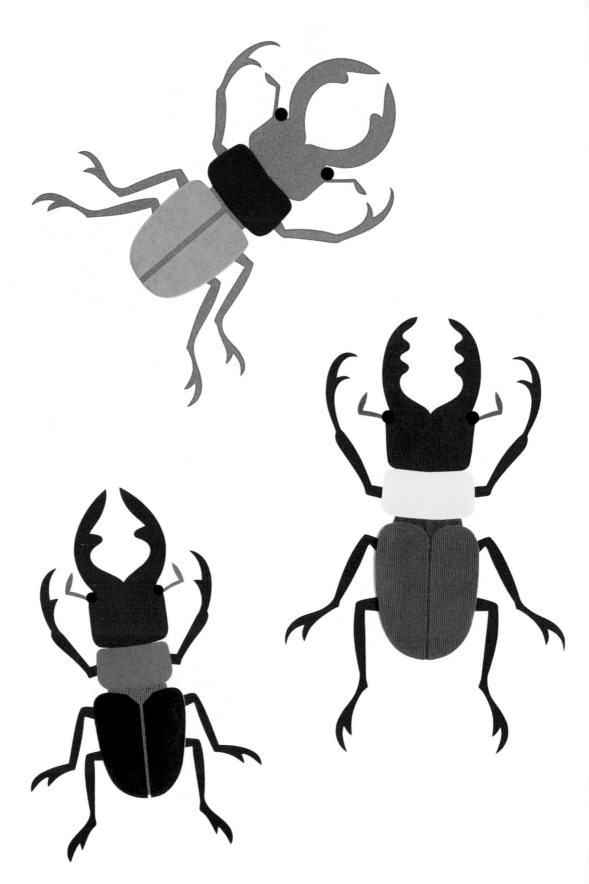

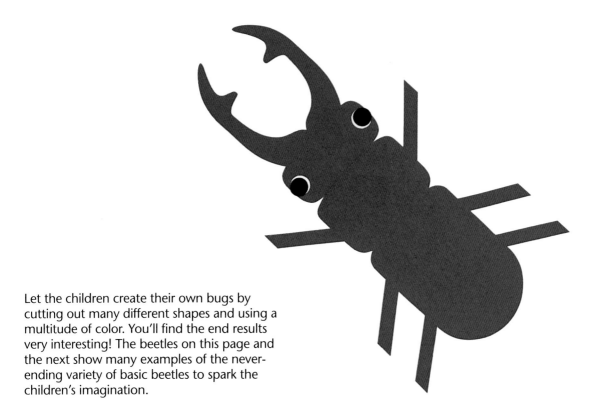

Let the children create their own bugs by cutting out many different shapes and using a multitude of color. You'll find the end results very interesting! The beetles on this page and the next show many examples of the never-ending variety of basic beetles to spark the children's imagination.

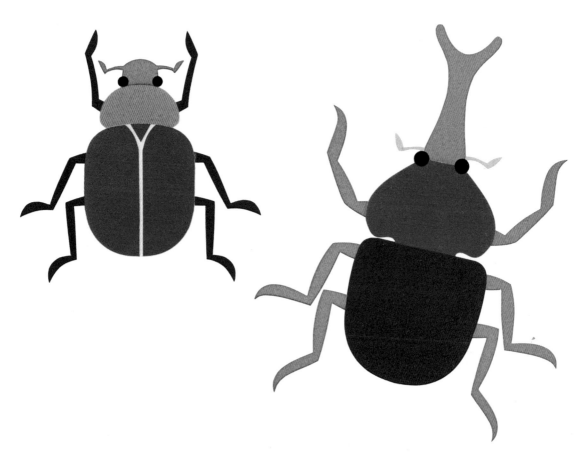

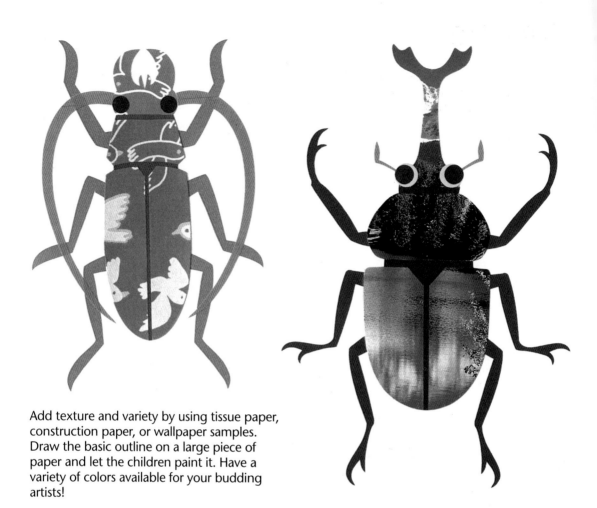

Add texture and variety by using tissue paper, construction paper, or wallpaper samples. Draw the basic outline on a large piece of paper and let the children paint it. Have a variety of colors available for your budding artists!

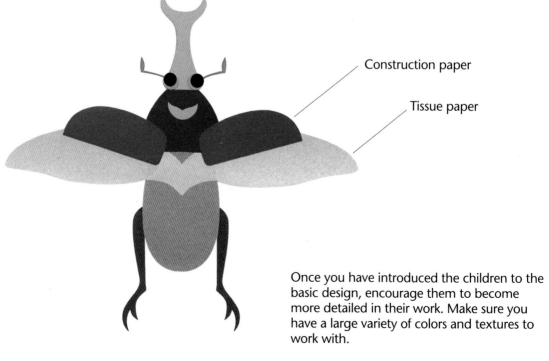

Construction paper

Tissue paper

Once you have introduced the children to the basic design, encourage them to become more detailed in their work. Make sure you have a large variety of colors and textures to work with.

Name Tags

In your studies of nature and insects why not make name tags for the children from these zany worms and caterpillars. This worm is basic enough so that the youngest child can do it. After they have completed their masterpieces take a black magic marker and write their name across the body.

MATTHEW

Briana

David

JOSEPH

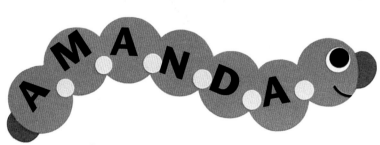

AMANDA

Spider Webs

Make a giant spider web from string or nylon fishing line in one corner of the room. Attach your spiders, some hanging, and some sitting on the "web".

Use bright colors and make many different varieties.

Coloring Contests

The cicada is another interesting insect. You can add these suspended from the ceiling to use bright colors!

See how many color combinations the children can come up with for this very colorful grasshopper.

After the children have colored these lady bugs, add some dimension by using holes from a hole puncher. The children will enjoy adding the spots and they will have fun trying to pick the tiny dots and glue them down.

Make a large beehive using a balloon as a base and cover it with papier maché. After the papier maché dries, pop the balloon, paint and hang from the ceiling. Attach the bees to a string and have them "buzzing" around the hive!

CHAPTER 3
BIRDS

Children are fascinated with birds. Their unique colors and ability to fly only enhance this fascination.

Add birds to many different themes and subjects. Jungles, zoos. ponds, meadows, oceans, and farms are just some of the different settings to choose from. Use the examples in this chapter to enhance and extend learning while on field trips to the zoo, local farm, etc. Adding far-out colors brightens any room. Children will love to create a "theme" bulletin board for each new subject studied.

Potato Prints

A great way to work with birds and teach a new skill is to use potato prints. Cutting the potatoes in half and tracing around the designs will give the children the ability to make many prints or use many colors. Some of the prints below are very basic while other ones are quite elaborate.

Instead of using potatoes for printing, you can pick up the sponges in craft stores that are flat and cut out the designs of the birds. The children may get a little messier, but the more elaborate designs can be achieved a lot easier.

Some are fancy and some are simple!

There are many varieties to choose from for a basic bird pattern.

Use a variety of colors or use just one!

Make a dramatic picture by using black or dark construction paper and light-colored paints. While the paint is still wet, sprinkle silver glitter around the edges of the wings to outline them.

There is no end to the ways in which these prints can be used. Add to the background of a "Day at the Park" or use these sea gulls to add to a "Day at the beach".

Use many different colors of paints in shallow dishes so the children can experiment with the colors. Backgrounds can be drawn on first with chalk. Then using 2 parts liquid starch and 1 part water, mix and paint onto the chalk drawing and let dry. This seals the chalk and makes it permanent. Then the children are free to add their birds over the drawing.

Add birds to the horizon. Notice the plants in the background can be glued on or can also be printed on with the potato prints, made in the same way as the birds.

Room Borders

Make a border around the room with a variety of flamingos.

You can either put the names of the children on them, or make one for each day of the week. Another idea is to make different colored ones for each month of the year. Any way you use them, it will brighten up your room!!

Farm and Forest Birds

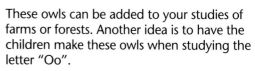

These owls can be added to your studies of farms or forests. Another idea is to have the children make these owls when studying the letter "Oo".

As you can see, you can make the same bird basic or fancy. Have the shapes cut out for the very young or traced and ready to cut to be glued together. The older ones can do it all!

Use these chickens and roosters when
studying farm life and farms.

As you can see there are many varieties to
choose from!!

Add these ducks and swan to your farm scene floating on a nearby pond.

Helper's Displays

The basic design of the bird can be used in a variety of art projects, mobiles, flying around the room, or sitting in a tree.

Why not have the children all make their own unique bird and use them in a Helper's Display. Using a basic tree design you can create an attractive display for the children to use.

By having the children help make the display, they can really feel involved in the finished project and the daily running of the classroom. This encourages responsibility and following directions.

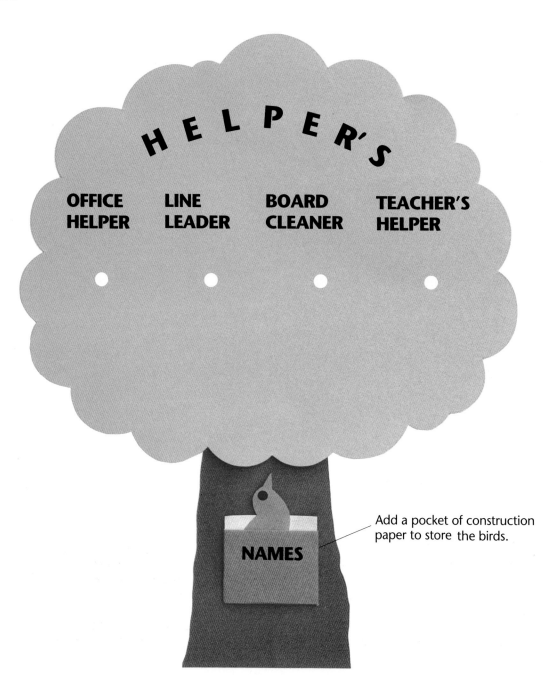

OFFICE HELPER   LINE LEADER   BOARD CLEANER   TEACHER'S HELPER

NAMES

Add a pocket of construction paper to store the birds.

Let the children pick which bird they want to be and have them laminated after writing the child's name on it. Then at the beginning of each day, pick a new set of "Helper's". There are many to choose from. You can use these titles or pick some of your own. Make sure to punch a hole at the top of the birds so you can hang them on push pins.

Whichever bird the children choose encourage them to use their imagination. Remind them to do their best work so they will be proud to display their handiwork for all to see.

Make sure to change the display with the change of the season or even the change of the month.

Danny

Manny

Michael

Toni

Achievement Award Displays

Using the pictures below you can create a beautiful classroom decoration the children can add to and be proud of as they achieve a new goal. Since every child has their own strengths and weaknesses academically, it is only logical that the theme of the display should change periodically. For example, the first month the theme could be math (ie:additon, subtraction, etc.) spelling, or reading, etc. The other alternative is to use it for more basic goals such as manners.

As the child achieves his or her goal they would add a new decoration to the tail or a new feather to the peacock. As the themes change the child would be allowed to bring the tail or feathers home for the parents to admire. This way all of the children can share in the limelight and feel special.

Encourage the children to use their
imagination and create their own unique bird.

On each new feather or decoration you can indicate what the child achieved, for example, "I can multiply by 2" or "#1 Speller for the week or September 12th, etc."

Bulletin Boards

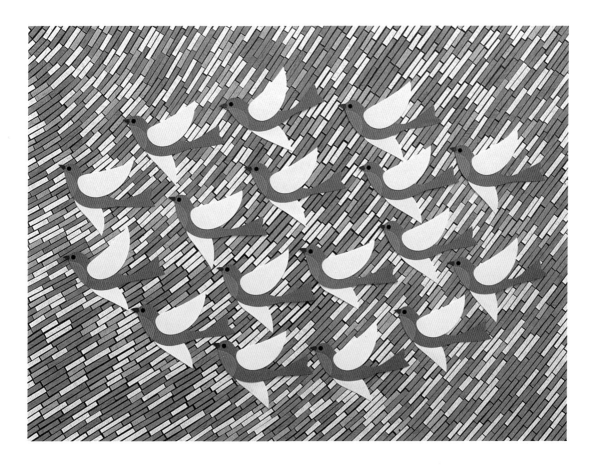

You can create a dramatic bulletin board from birds that are all the same or all different. The background is nothing more than cut pieces of paper in the same color scheme that creates a dramatic background rather than the standard plain sheets of colored construction paper. To do this is a time consuming operation but the background can be used over and over again.

A new and different way to display the birds is to have the children make trees to suspend from the ceiling or attach to the wall around the room.

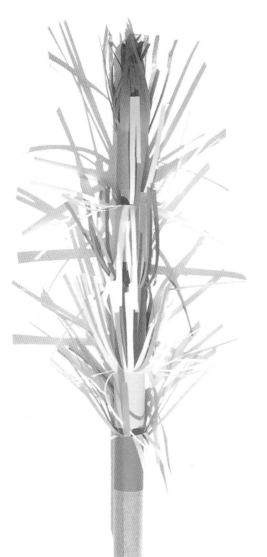

First roll up some brown paper into a tube to form the tree trunk. Next fringe several pieces of green paper, using a variety of shades of green. Wrap these around the "tree trunk" and attach with glue. Let the green fringe hang down to create the foliage.

81

CHAPTER 4

OTHER FIGURES

Transportation

There are many different modes of transportation. Cars, trucks, buses, and bicycles are seen frequently in a child's life. Open up their world to other kinds of transportation such as trains, hot air balloons, trams, helicopters and boats.

You can start with buses. School buses and city buses are everyday sights in most parts of the country. But how many children think of the double decker buses in England?

While studying the different kinds of transportation, why not have the children's name tags made from these air trams? You can use all of the same colors or make each one different and unique as each child is different and unique.

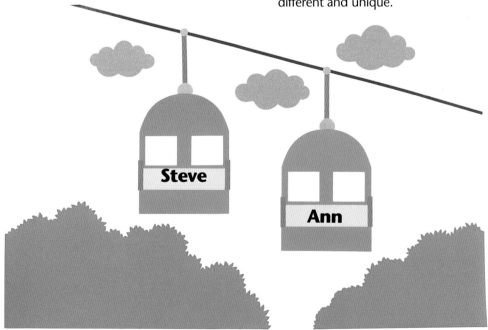

Here is a hot air balloon that is easily reproduced. The children can make them from brightly colored construction paper and use them as name tags or make them three dimensional with papier maché and suspend them from the ceiling around the room.

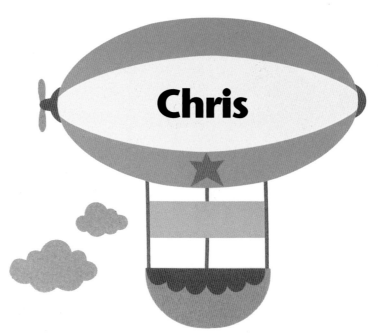

Chris

To make the three dimensional hot air balloons, have the children cover a large ballon with strips of newspaper dipped in paste. Let the balloon dry and then have the children paint them as they choose. Make the balloons fancy by adding stars, stripes, hearts, or logos from local businesses. Add string to attach the basket.

For the basket you can do one of two things. Either use the plastic baskets found in the fresh produce department of the supermarkets and let the children weave paper through the holes or let the children weave their own out of construction paper. Cut the paper that is to be used for the base to the desired size and then fold in half length wise. Next cut the paper from the folded side 3/4 of the way across and then open up and you are ready to start weaving. Have strips cut for the children to use to do the weaving.

Starting at one side, let the children weave the paper strips in and out of the base, and repeat the process until the base is full. Next, glue the strips to the base at the top and bottom to secure them. After this dries, you can trim off the excess so that they are even with the base.

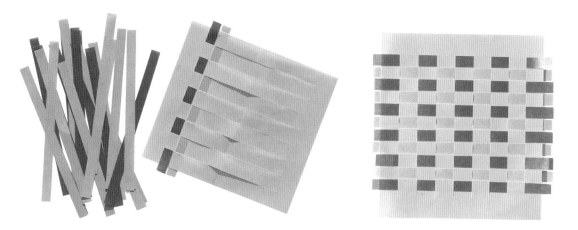

You can use contrasting colors to make the basket more festive or you can use coordinating colors to match your balloons. Make sure to push all of the strips together for a tight weave before gluing. After your baskets have dried, fold them into a rectangle shape and staple together. Cut a rectangle from construction paper that is slightly bigger than the folded basket and attach it to form the bottom of the basket. Attach to the bottom of the basket and suspend them from the ceiling around the room.

Another way to learn about transportation is to let the children reproduce these trains. The children will also brush up on using their shapes as well. Have a model as an example but encourage the children to add their own personal style.

Circles, squares, triangles, rectangles, half circles, etc. are cut from colored construction paper and the children can pick the ones they want to create their masterpieces!

Have a variety of shapes already cut out for the children to choose from and place in separate baskets to keep them organized and available to the children.

You can make the trains more realistic by adding background buildings or bushes.

Here is another mode of transportation the childen are familiar with. Planes and helicopters are seen everywhere - either around the area or on the television. These can be reproduced easily and they are basic enough for even the youngest of children. Encourage the children to add their own details. (ie: stripes, stars, numbers, etc.)

Let the children make these sailboats and add finishing touches such as waves, clouds, or potato printed sea gulls.

For a wild change let the children create their own Viking ships and encourage the children to use their imagination and add their own personal style.

For a festive change why not explore the different modes of transportation at a carnival. These merry-go-round horses would make a bright room border and you can let each child make a different colored one. Add the poles, made either from strips of construction paper or tubes from wrapping paper and add a giant top to encompass all of the horses.

Any child who has gone to a carnival or seen one on television will remember the airplanes that they rode in that went up into the air and then back down again.

Calendars

Instead of buying a calendar display for the room you can make one and let the children help. Use a large piece of poster board in a color of your choice and draw the basic calendar grid.

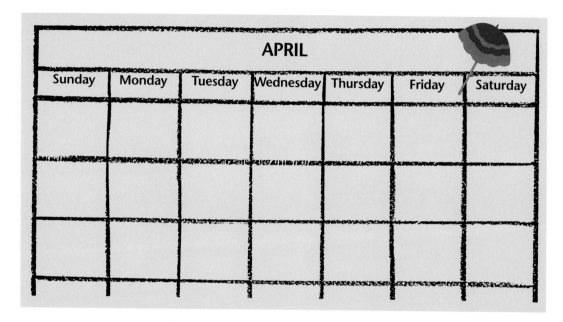

You can use these pictures below to be used as numbers on the calendar. I have given some examples of months to correspond with the pictures.

January

March

May

April

April

For March you could use the shape of the shamrock or something similar but whatever you choose for each month, make sure that you laminate or cover each one with clear contact paper for use year after year.

Another thought is to attach an envelope under the calendar to store all of the unused symbols.

June

August

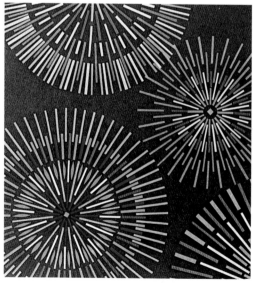

July

August

October

September

December

December

International Bazaars

A fantastic way to interest the children in Social Studies is to involve them in an International Bazaar. Study the culture of a specific country in depth and give each group or class a different country or continent to study. (ie: Japan, France, Germany, Italy, Greece, Switzerland, Australia, etc.)

Have the children decorate the classroom and fashion costumes to be worn at the bazaar which is held at the end of a specified period of time (2 weeks, 1 month).

Also study the native foods and make a snack to be sampled by the students at the bazaar. Allow the children to tour each of the classrooms and visit all of the different "countries". The children will be excited to decorate their countries!

If your classroom is studying Japan, for example, you can prepare a different project for each day.

Monday: Japanese Lanterns (1)
Cherry Blossom Trees (2)

Tuesday: Write Japanese Names (3)
Start Kimonos (4)

Wednesday: Finish Kimonos (5)
Origami (6)

Thursday: Pictures of Mt. Fuji (7)
Fish Kites (8)

Friday: Japanese Boys and
Japanese Girls (9-10)

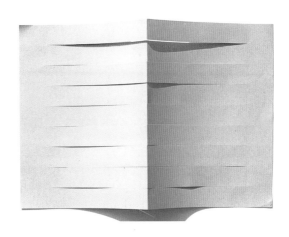

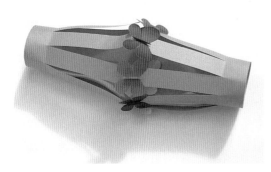

(1) Lanterns are easy and fast to make. Using 8½ x 11 piece of construction paper, fold in half lengthwise and make cutlines 3/4 of the way across for the children to cut.

After the children have cut the paper, open it up and roll to form the lantern. Decorate them with flowers and butterflies and hang them around the room.

(2) Cherry blossom trees are easy using a base piece of construction paper. Have the children glue real twigs onto the base paper. Then glue pink pieces of tissue paper to form the blossoms around the tree. The bulletin board can also be turned into a three dimensional masterpiece!

(3) Children would love to have Japanese names for the week. Research the language and find the names for each child and how to write it in Japanese. Then let the children write their names on white pieces of butcher paper cut into strips with black paint. For the smaller children you may have to trace the Japanese letters lightly with pencil for them to copy over. Hang your name banners as name tags for the children.

As part of your studies of the country of your choice you can learn certain words and use them during the week (ie: hello, good bye, please, thank you, etc.)

(4) The picture above can be reproduced using scraps of wallpaper, but in order for the children to wear them plastic bags are the better solution.

To make the kimonos for the children, start with a large plastic bag, unfolded. Slit up the sides of the bag from the opening to the folded bottom.

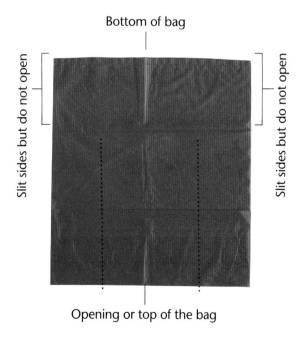

Bottom of bag

Slit sides but do not open

Slit sides but do not open

Opening or top of the bag

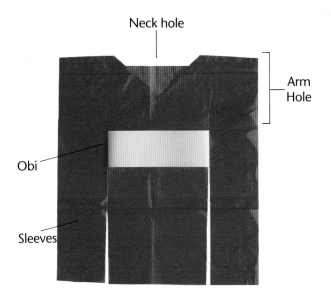

Neck hole

Arm Hole

Obi

Sleeves

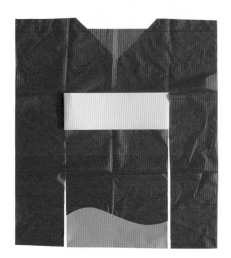

Next cut along the dotted lines through both layers of the bag to form the sleeves.

After this cut up the middle (through the top layer only) and make a "v" cut at the top of the bag to form the neck hole.

Glue the top of the bog to the bottom of the bag between the marks to form the sides and sleeves. This reinforces the sideseams – Otherwise they will rip open through use. Then add decorations such as flowers or Japanese writing to the Komono. Fashion an obi or belt from contrasting colors. There are garbage bags for all sizes of children!

For the girls in the class you can use flowers and butterflies for decoration and for the boys in the class you can use Japanese characters, fish or cranes as decoration.

(5) To complete the costumes you can make Japanese shoes from heavy cardboard and rubber bands. Trace an outline of the children's feet onto a piece of cardboard. Don't forget to mark the initials of the children on both of the shoes.

Use a razor knife to cut out the shoes. After cutting out the shoes, punch out holes to form a triangle at the top of the shoes for the rubber bands.

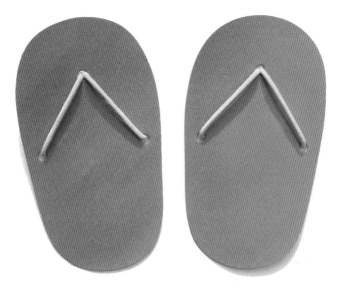

Cut the rubber band to form a strip of rubber and lace into the holes. Attach with staples or tie a knot. Make certain that the bands are not too tight so the children can wear them without cutting off their circulation.

For the fans you can use popsicle sticks and heavy paper. Decorate them with flowers to match the girls' kimonos.

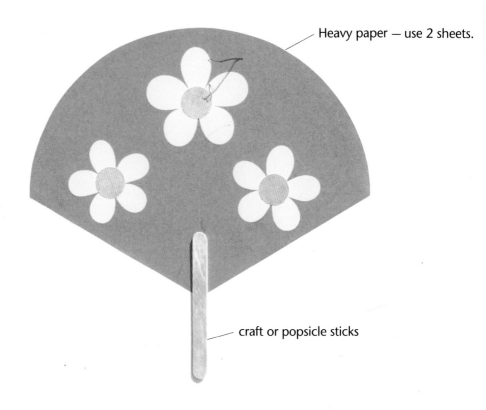

Heavy paper — use 2 sheets.

craft or popsicle sticks

For the swords you can use heavy cardboard covered with tin foil. Attach a long piece of string to tie the swords around the boys' waists.

(6) Origami is fun for children of all ages.
Research the different types and pick out a
few different designs for your age group. The
children will love practicing this art project!!

Fold the square of
colored paper corner
to corner, twice.

Open one of the triangular pockets
and fold corner to corner, making
a square. Do the same with the
reverse side, matching the squares.

Fold one of the open
sides to the middle.

Do the same with the
reverse.

Unfold and open.
Flatten to create a
rhombus.

Do the same on the
reverse side.

Fold both front and
reverse sides inward to
middle. It is important
to fold edges precisely.
Fold back the neck portion.

Fold back the tail
portion in the same
way. Fold back a small
portion of the neck to
create the head. Finally,
blow air into the hole in
the belly to inflate the
crane.

(7) Have the children recreate these pictures
of Mt. Fuji to hang up in the room.

(8) Kites are very traditional art forms in Japan. They are very easy for the children to create and show off. As you can see from the picture below, they are a very colorful addition to the room. On the next few pages you will find instructions as well as diagrams to follow.

Cut out a fish form from two large pieces of tissue paper. Be sure to square off the mouth to have a place to put the oak tag strips.

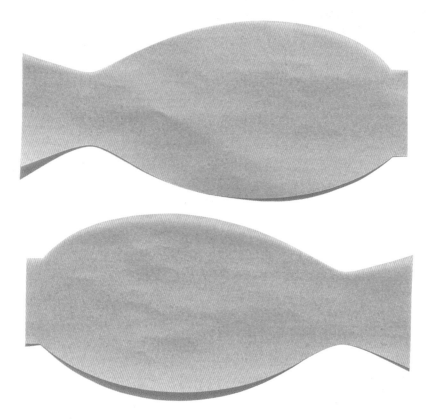

After cutting out the form, glue the sides of the fish excluding the mouth. Cut a thin strip of oak tag 11/2 times the size of the mouth and roll to form a circle. Staple oak tag circle and then place inside mouth of the fish. Fold the tissue paper around the oak tag and glue.

Tissue covered oak tag

Now you are ready to cut out the details and add them to your kites. Have eyes, fins, scales, etc. to add to the fish. Let dry and then punch 2 holes to attach string for hanging. You can hang them from thin dowels for fishing poles or traditional bamboo.

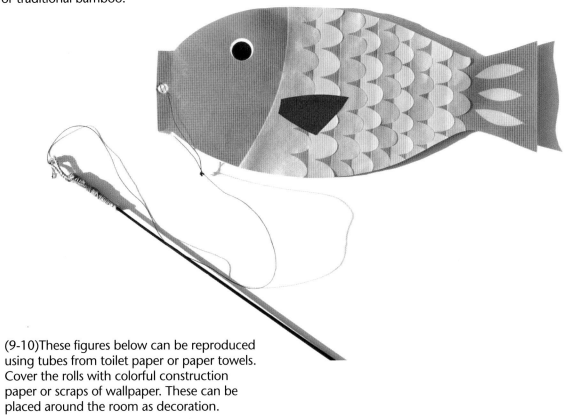

(9-10)These figures below can be reproduced using tubes from toilet paper or paper towels. Cover the rolls with colorful construction paper or scraps of wallpaper. These can be placed around the room as decoration.

Farmers Bazaar

When studying nutrition you can turn a dull unit into an experience the children will not soon forget.

In addition to studying food groups and nutrition you can help the children start their own fruit/vegetable garden. Assign a fruit or vegetable to each student and have them bring in a package of seeds to share with the class.

Plant the seeds in small baby food jars and have the children mark the jars with the name of the seeds planted in the jar. You can have the children make plant markers to bring home and use in their gardens when the seeds have sprouted. With everyone contributing in the class, you should have a large variety of plants to choose from. If there is available window space you can continue the garden in the room and assign plant care and maintenance to the students.

Use the fruits and vegetables below as an example for the plant markers.

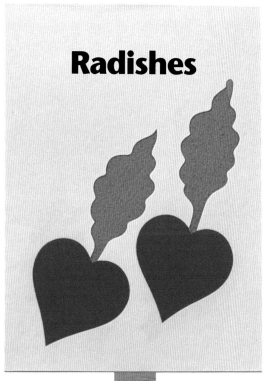

Using poster board as a base let the children decorate the markers with crayons or make the vegetables from construction paper and glue onto the poster board. Cover with clear contact paper or laminate and then glue on craft sticks.

As a display in the classroom you can make a giant fruit and vegetable stand to display all of the fruits and vegetables the children have made.

Let the children make pictures of their favorite food and display them in the room. If you use your imagination there are many to choose from.

A simple way to enhance your study of the dairy food group is to make home made butter. Using small jars (ie. baby food) pour a small amount of heavy cream and cover tightly. Allow the children to shake the jars until the contents becomes solid. Chill and serve with saltine crackers. Discuss the difference between this butter and store bought butter. You'll surprise them with this fun idea!

At the end of this unit you can plan a special breakfast or luncheon for the children or invite the parents and have the children serve their respective parents. Send out special invitations and have the children volunteer to bring different dishes of food and have a pot-luck lunch. For breakfast you can have eggs, bacon, sausage, biscuits, doughnuts, french toast, waffles, etc. For lunches you can have sandwiches, mini pizzas, chips, dip, fresh vegetables and dip, "friendship fruit salad" etc. There is a lot to choose from if the children use their imagination and bring a special family recipe that they like.

CHAPTER 5

FAIRY TALES

Children love fairy tales. Reading the story to the children is wonderful, but why not let the children become involved in the process.

Create a felt board on the back of a book case or make it more portable by covering an old board. Next ceate new pictures by making them out of felt or by making them out of paper and attaching felt or flannel to the back. Now the children can use a whole set of pictures to tell a story and the children can help with putting pictures up on the board.

This can also be used as a center once in a while for a special treat. Collect a lot of different pictures and let the child create their own story. This will enhance their own creativity and encourage them to use their own imagination. For the older child, you can make a game out of this. Give each child a different picture making sure they are from different stories. Then you start the story. Call on the children to add their own parts to the story from the picture they are holding. Not only will the results be quite funny, but the children are using their imagination.

The Emperor's New Clothes

The Three Little Pigs

A Wolf and the Seven Goats

The Little Mermaid

On the next several pages you will find many pictures that can be used in conjunction with the rest of the ideas in this book. They are divided into groups such as Animals, Birds, Insects, Fish and Sea Life, Flowers and Nature, Fairy Tales and Fantasia and Hari-E Works. I hope you will be as inspired as I was.

117

119

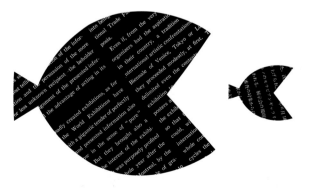

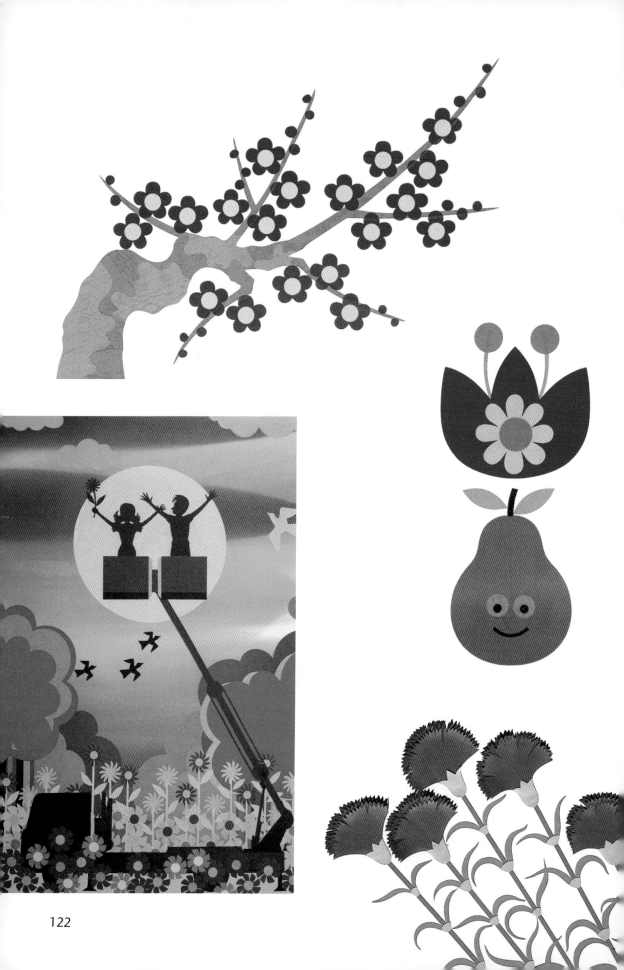

Hari-E Works

Presented here are works of Hari-E, pasted paper pictures with mosaic backgrounds. The explanation of the process for creating Hari-E is simple. The example below begins with the background. Using pieces of paper in the shape of tiles a mosaic is laid out. When this is done, the largest element of the picture is then pasted up, followed by the smaller elements. In short, smaller pieces are laid over larger pieces. By mixing paper cut with scissors and cutters with paper torn by hand, and by pasting pieces more or less loosely to the paper, one can achieve three-dimensional and other effects. Please experiment. Use tweezers to paste on such details as the part of the child's face.

127

Masami Hanamura

1944   Born in Negishi, Taito Ward, Tokyo.
1956   Graduates from Kanasogi Elementary
        School.
1960   Graduates from Shitaya Junior High
        School.
1963   Graduates from Uenoshinobugaoka
        High School.
        Entered Kan'eijizaka Arts School
1966   Becomes freelance designer.

Exhibits:
Ginza Matsuya (1963), Nishi-Ginza
Department Store (1968), Mitsubishi Sky Ring
(1970), Odakyu Department (1972), Sony
Building (1977), Ginza San'ai (1978, 1980),
Odakyu Hark (1982), Tokyo Daimaru
Department (1984), Seibu Department Store
Shibuya (1984), Yokohama Center Building
(1984), Chujitsuya Isehara Bene (1986),
others.

Books:
"Kiri-E Hari-E (Ohayo Publishing), "Colorful
Cut Collection" Fancy Cut Collection"
(Graphic-sha Publishing).

Address:
2-24-1-506 Nishi-Sugamo,
Toshima-ku, Tokyo 170
Japan
Tel. 03-3576-0266

Wendy Jones

Wendy Jones as a teacher's aide, brings to this
book her expertise and knowledge of exciting
and multifaceted uses for Mr. Hanamura's
wonderful cut collections. She now lives in
Texas, and began working in a Day School in
1984 with pre-schoolers, turning the
classroom into a creative atmosphere for
hands-on learning and a place for
imaginations to grow.
She is a wife and mother of three children
herself, ages 12, 10 and 5, and uses her talent
in their daily lives as well.